THE DARK BETWEEN THE TWILIGHT

A Journey Through Evil, Loneliness, and Redemption

JAMAL HODGE

Let the world know:
#IGotMyCLPBook!

Crystal Lake Publishing
www.CrystalLakePub.com

WELCOME
TO ANOTHER

CRYSTAL LAKE PUBLISHING
CREATION

Join today at www.crystallakepub.com & www.patreon.com/CLP

This book is dedicated to the woman that carried my body &
spirit to birth, nurtured my love & my pain, and taught me that
Mother is more than human but less than God. Mother is the
muse of life. I love you, Mom.

SPECIAL THANKS TO:

My editor, mentor, and friend, **Linda D. Addison,** who lifted me up by the ankles, flipped me upside down, and shook me until all the pretense, self-doubt, and lies fell out of my pockets. Leaving only what's real. From her, I have learned that it is far better to be vulnerable in your writing than to be clever.

To my sister, **Kyeisha Hodge,** who has been the loudest advocate of my affliction, the curse to write. Thank you for enduring the purgatory of first drafts and the strange calls fueled by my panicked ego, *"Does it work?"*, *"Is it good?"*, *"But is it REALLY good?"* Hopefully, this final draft will make amends.

To the people that hurt me, and to those I've scarred along the way. Know that the pain inflicted led me to the right questions. In many ways, this book of poetry is one of the answers I received.

I love you all.

PRAISE FOR
THE DARK BETWEEN THE TWILIGHT

Hodge's poetry uses the language of every day and classical to create beautiful new songs. Wielding this unique instrument, he takes us on a journey, through space & time, to show life surviving in the harsh realities of justice denied, love refused, ghosts haunted, and infinite cosmos honored. There is growth and beauty reflected in the ashes of human weakness, in poems that unwind like a prayer to show how awakened choice can make destiny self-evident. This is a book to be read more than once, so that unexpected layers can be revealed.

—Linda D. Addison,
award-winning author, HWA Lifetime Achievement Award recipient and SFPA Grand Master.

Jamal Hodge invites us to dive deep into our emotions to experience what it truly means to live. His latest collection *The Dark Between the* Twilight is an introspective look into the dichotomy of existence and existing. His words are raw, powerful, and unforgettable. They stay with you on this darkly haunting journey into the human condition.

—Christina Sng,
Bram Stoker Award winning author of
A Collection of Nightmares

If you haven't read *The Dark Between the Twilight*, you're missing out on a marvelous collection by Jamal Hodge, a new poet of many talents. The book consists of three sections, and each holds a wonderment all its own. Hodge is a genius at bringing you into his world with Poems of an intimately personal level, mixed in with a selection of speculative poems to entice the imagination.

—Marge Simon,
Multiple Stoker Award recipient, and SFPA award winner

The Dark Between the Twilight is a voice vibrating beneath the skin, remembering the oblivion of something too little—ourselves—and the huge shadows at the end of the tunnel, with diamonds for eyes—lures, promises. That voice tells about our lives of flesh, the universe, and all the splinters running fast between them. A book to read.

—Alessandro Manzetti,
3x Bram Stoker Award winner and Elgin Award winner

"Every now and then, the world is introduced to a work of art that transcends without end; that is not bound to time nor space but rather collective consciousness itself. With soul-wrenching poems such as 'The Dream of Worms' and 'Tomorrow, I'll Be Five', or the vulnerability of 'Goodbye', and the affecting 'Stay. Live.', Jamal's book, *The Dark Between the Twilight*, touches upon a reader's enigmatic soul with an introspective emotion that will inspire generations of artists to come."

—Nzondi,
Bram Stoker Award-winning Author

From the dedication to the way Jamal Hodge ends this collection is beautifully brilliant. Hodge uses his unique talent to create more than a collection of poetry and prose. He grants a glimpse at his innermost thoughts, doubts, and often harsh reality. This profound way of thinking and writing allows for a connection with the reader on a new level, which leads you to ask these questions of one's self.
—Cindy O'Quinn,
Rhysling & Dwarf Star Nominated Poet and
two-time Bram Stoker Award nominee.

The Dark Between the Twilight explores how beauty can be found in sorrow, how pain can lead to strength. Each page unfolds like a vision, both breathtaking and heart-wrenching. Jamal Hodge boldly spills his blood for us, reaching, as the best poets do, for the unvarnished truth of who he is and the bitter challenges we all face. You can't read this collection and not be changed."
—Brian W. Matthews,
author of the *Forever Man* series

TABLE OF CONTENTS

FOREWORD

I WAS INTRODUCED to Jamal Hodge, a writer, filmmaker, poet, and visionary, by Horror Grandmaster Linda D. Addison, and given that Addison is a supernatural spirit, an oracle of truth when it comes to souls in whom the darkness spools, I did not hesitate to say yes. Within days, we had arranged a Zoom date, the two of us communing over coffee, oceans, and time zones. As a soothsayer, Addison knows her craft; I discovered a kindred spirit in that hour, Hodge and I playing a game of literary snap, laying down card after card of shared experience and belief. We talked of community, collaborations, and constructivism. When the hour was up, I was thirsty for more, so Hodge kindly gifted me this book, *The Dark Between the Twilight*, his not-yet-published debut poetry collection, describing it as "an exercise in coming out of abuse and depression towards restoration and life."

"I hope it connects with you," he wrote, his humility stark on the page.

Shouldering my own stories of assault and depression, I immersed myself in the poet's words.

I'm glad I did. It's an exquisite collection. Addison is right when she says Hodge's poems "unwind like a prayer.' Discovering *The Dark Between the Twilight* was like advancing down a dark cavern, stepping gingerly from poem to poem, towards an uncertain destination. Two poems, both with the word "perhaps" in the title, provided landmarks, a welcome juxtaposition of fear and hope. With their recurring rhythm and repetition, these poems reveal some of the poet's transformation in the writing of this work and highlight an ongoing desire for self-evaluation and awareness.

The collection is grouped into three sections, loosely delivered to themes, or perhaps chronologically according to the stages of his self-actualization, and features Hodge's reflections on hell

("Songs of the Night"), vulnerability ("A Black Scream in the Twilight"), and on honesty ("A Song of Dawn"). Largely written during 2020, the year of the new coronavirus, certain poems hint at global and national events—the isolation of the pandemic and instances of social and political unrest—while others deliver sharp observations from the poet's quotidian, with images as vivid as postcards. Throughout, we're aware of Hodge's compassion and his rage.

There are no false starts in *The Dark Between the Twilight*. Particular favorites include "The Dying Girl" and "Alone," both achingly lonely pieces, which spoke to me of isolation, otherness, and depression. "I'm Sorry," with its scathing unrepentant purgatory, is another highlight.

Why must we despise those who try to love us? the poet asks. Why indeed?

In *The Dark Between the Twilight*, we are confronted with moments of breathtaking realism: for example, in childhood dreams of breakdancing on the moon ("Foster Child"); in the "unbroken chain of generations" ("Happy Birthday"), and in unloved souls who "suckle vinegar" from Cruelty's bosom ("Unloved"). In these and other fleeting images, Hodge deftly manipulates language and sound.

As you would expect from a filmmaker, shape and form also play a role in Hodge's work. There is the startling simplicity of words embodied in the shape of "Waves," a poem which crashes on the paper, whereas "Sanctioned" is cinched tight to the center of the page, and we see in "The Bridge Above their Walls" the bold connecting struts in the structure of the poem. There is "In the Right," with its deliberate right-facing arrowhead form, reflecting the fierce conviction of its narrator, and in "Everybody Dies," the chilling refrain is a brutal reminder to readers of the eternal cycle of life and death.

The final poem in the collection, "Restoration," is a collaboration with Hodge's sister and supporter, Kyeisha Hodge. Rather than being out of place, this collaborative work offers a poignant high note to round out the collection's overarching melody.

Readers can't help but bring their own experience to a poem, finding their own meanings in the perfect arrangement of words or even the unsaid things that seep out from between the lines. For me, "Siblings" was such a poem. It shook me, making my ribs ache with its candor and revealing an unflinching truth that those of us blessed (and cursed) with siblings understand and yet often cannot voice. I last saw my sister in the hour after my father's death. Since then, more than two years on, her grief has been an impenetrable scribble between us. With all our past entanglements, all those unpickable nitpickings, I can find no way through. Hodge gets it. He's lived it. "It's all gone insane," he states, capturing the hurt. *Sibling, enemy, friend.* Perhaps, when it is published, I'll send my sister a copy of this work, letting Hodge voice the truth that I cannot, so my much-loved baby sister might yet hold 'my wrinkled hand' at the end. Because poetry has that power, doesn't it? To heal and to restore, its "meaning, carved into darkness" ("Restoration," Hodge & Hodge).

North Carolina poet Alice Osborn says, "Poetry is like the Windex on a grubby car window," claiming, "it bares open the vulnerabilities of human beings, so we can all relate to each other a little better." In *The Dark Between the Twilight*, Jamal Hodge eviscerates himself. He lays himself bare; he conducts a forthright conversation with the reader, a heartfelt testimony of revelation, recognition, and restoration, from the moving words he pens in his dedication and acknowledgements that preface this book, to the final assertion in his biographical notes, an everyman promise of a better self. And at the end, at the conclusion of this journey of restoration, he fancies himself a pretty cool guy.

Jamal Hodge is definitely a pretty cool guy. I invite you all to discover the poet and his work in the pages of this haunting collection, where, from the darkness, his light escapes as scintillating pinpricks of hope.

Lee Murray, October 2022

Reference:

Osborn, A. (2016). *Why poetry is important to our world today.* Retrieved from: https://aliceosborn.com/why-is-poetry-important-to-our-world-today/

INTRODUCTION

STARVED FOR HUMAN TOUCH, dismissive of the relevance of every effort in the face of death, the year 2020 left me somewhere between cold numbness and burning sadness, as unmotivated as the slaughterhouse animal.

As always, I retreated to the thorny garden of words for my salvation. This collection is my rickety cathedral of prose. Here, as Virgil guided Dante, I invite you to transverse these quiet songs of darkness, this Purgatory of Twilight, and accept the bright prism of Heavenly contradiction.

This journey through extremity saved me from my own terrors. Poems born in truest love and despair, lend them your eye, lend them your ear . . .

A SONG OF NIGHT

Evil is not the opposite of good, but its absence. The void is devoid of compassion or true community, where the light of creation is eclipsed by the needs of the self. And as the black hole swallows ceaselessly, so too does the hollow soul. Ever unsatisfied. Empty.

The poems in this section explore this Hell that I often find myself banished to by my own hand. The acts taken, the words spoken, the good left undone. In darkness, I learn to appreciate the light.

PERHAPS...

Perhaps, God has no motive,
Perhaps, Man is a slave to Fate,
Perhaps, your faith came way too fucking late.

Perhaps, this is Heaven,
Perhaps, the wicked enjoy Hell,
Perhaps, the dead feel everything but are unable to tell.

Perhaps, this is just a simulation, nothing you love is real.
Perhaps, at the end of the day, that's not such a big deal.

Perhaps, ideas had you before you had ideas.
Perhaps, everything is legitimate about your fears.

Perhaps, we are the midwives of higher intelligences to come.
Perhaps, serial killers are having the most fun.

Perhaps, after proving yourself a waste of sperm and time,
Even your own mother would name you a stain upon the ass of
swine.

Perhaps, the haters are right!
Perhaps, you still manage to sleep all cozy at night.
Perhaps, I offended you, got under your thin skin.
Perhaps, God wants none of us to win.

Perhaps this and perhaps that,
Perhaps,
nothing I told you is a fact.

Or perhaps ...

THE GREAT BLUE STOMACH
THAT CIRCLES THE SUN

I cry often,
in great mewling heaves,
with the revelation of cyclical doom.
The inescapable knowledge
of what mortality means,
for breathing things
born within the licking whirlwind.

Violence is the architect of historic grandeur.
Why, then, do we pretend the flower is without thorns,
and little things born
will not grow teeth?

All devours.
Life eats life.
But propagates itself to keep the feast eternal.

Pause to consider,
energy can't be destroyed,

4

just recycled.
Energy and matter are the same.
The mass of the world does not change with a species' extinction.
Flesh is given to new forms.
New mouths,
new stomachs.
Feast upon feast.

Where!
Oh, where,
is God to declare us good?

The world is but a stomach.
The meaning of life is teeth.
One thing,
thinking it's many,
endlessly digesting itself.

The great blue stomach that circles the sun.

UNLOVED

The unloved do not forgive.
Cruelty adopts us,
teaching knowledge,
without compassion,
as we suckle vinegar from
her shriveled bosom,
gripping talons that bleed small fingers,
laughed at when we cry.

Unwatered virtue
breeds a burning crop.
Our toil given
to every seed of hate.

Bleakness draws a counterfeit positivity,
adorned by fanged intentions.
Condemned, forever,
to the grim past,
whose muse is Inferno.

The sun sets behind our lost eyes,
the future, a lion's shadow.

Unloved,
Unwanted,
Unknown inside,
Hiding in pride to appear unbroken.
Holding the knife to life,
the dead,
amongst the dying.

XENOPHOBIA

A rainfall of tears at my cheeks,
storms of spittle flying free,
as my legs explore the limits
of their functionality.

Delirium . . . my delight,
in the rolling shimmer
of refracting ideas.

The duration of crying,
in the space of nothing
within my mind,
could flood eternity.

How sweet,
these disfigured pursuits
of senseless fruits.

Meaningless meanings
to warm our heads,
replaced quietly,
when the cracks begin to show.

Glass virtues,
sharp enough to draw spiritual blood.
Cutting me from me, the pieces fall
multi-colored as autumn leaves,
in a pile of terrors at my feet.

When hasn't my soul cried?
Perpetually mourning,
the thrice-blind mind,
of the completed fool.

A rainfall of tears at my cheeks,
storms of spittle flying free,
frantic legs take me nowhere.
There is nowhere they aren't.

Nowhere. Everywhere.

I am one of them.

MR. EGO

Mrs. Joy wore a mask of sorrows,
sitting on the grave I'd constructed
for that animal called Life,
who grieved,
bound as it were,
at my feet,
where I stood knee deep
in self-made wrongs.

And Mrs. Joy asked,
"Sir, am I not as you remember?"

So dug, I did,
much too fast.
In the frenzy of my shrinking world,
her wail became my laugh.

Life struggled at my feet,
mumbling distant promises,
bleeding lost hopes,
bound in chains carefully crafted
from the pain of my failures.

Where upon the horizon
stood Mr. Ego,
my only friend,
guiding my means to an end.

THE DREAM OF WORMS

A worm imagines itself a God:

in warm paths of mud,
worms remain worms.

A man imagines himself a king:

in warm paths of mud,
people become slaves.

Our gift:
this shared illusion,
to say this is that,
to name a place 'mine'
having others die,

to breed ideas
that serve one generation,
enslaving the rest,

to build boundaries
within the infinite minds
of our loves,

violent meanings
in shrinking hearts,
souring blood.

Are we demons?
Setting fire to our flesh
to cauterize our souls.

Or are we the dreaming worm,
thinking ourselves gods,
only to fall back into the mud,

and crawl . . .

ARTSCAPE OF EVILS

Burnt orgies of intolerant undoing,
the great unmaking,
demanding the degradation of beauty
in the unprecedented malice
of peculiar craftsmanship.

Continental gardens of a two-legged crop,
vomited forth in the violated image of God,
sprout ghastly imaginings of massacred flesh,
ascending mortal conceptions of Evil,

to howling art form, to baleful science.
Behold, the frightful method,
meticulous formulas perfected,
in the organic machinery of stitched organs.

Nauseous martyrs of willful vanity,
seduced to a one-sided affair,
sacrificed to horrid pleasure,
copulate without rest,
thrusting through grotesque transformations,
applied in living death.

The herded audience,
refined, through timeless degradation,
gazes upon unspeakable works
with unnamable sounds . . .

TOMORROW, I'LL BE FIVE

Inspired by Pulitzer Prize-winning photo "The Vulture and the little Girl" by Kevin Carter, 1994.

My skin is gaunt,
　　　　drawn tight to the skull.
My eyes are wide.
If I can make it,
Tomorrow, I'll be five.

No one will celebrate,
No one is left alive.
　　　　The tall men opened dad
To show us the pink stuff under the red.
　　　　Mom ran and lost half her head.
I gathered as much as I could carry of her in my pocket,
Before they sent me on my way.
The whole village was on fire.
The tall men said, "Have a nice day."

It gets hot out here.
          I drank from the water on the floor.
My stomach got sad,
          it hurts so bad,
I miss my mom,
I miss my dad.

Things are coming out of me,
In colors very bold.
Greens and browns,
Whites, and sticky gold,
They explode from my nose
          down my legs,
          from my frown.
The colors follow me
As I crawl across the ground.

What's the sun doing,
          why won't it go away?
It does things to my skin.
          It peels away.

Everything hurts.
          The flies are the worst.
          It seems they're here to stay.
Maybe they've come to celebrate?
My birthday is just a day away.

Sometimes the world goes off
          and comes back again.
I reach out and eat what I can.
          Dirt is salty,
          has no taste.
The predators who've seen me
Think I'm a waste.
Hard to move.
Easy to count my ribs.
I want to be five,
          but I wonder if I'll live.

Tomorrow, I'll be five.
        Where's Mom?
        Where's Dad?
I want to go where they are,
I want to go away.
I think I'm almost there.
The sudden sound makes me stay.
Thunder on the ground,
The sound of feet.
        People to meet.

I turn my head,
        it's all I can do.
Mom, Dad, is that you?

There's a man, pale as milk,
        and others too.
They look very sad.
        Are they hungry too?
I want to warn them to get away.
The tall men might come,
        to take important things away.
Rid them of their smiles,
Their pointing fingers
And curious glances.
Light flashes from the rectangles in their hands.
Some cry, none help.

My skin is gaunt,
        drawn tight to the skull.
        My eyes are wide.
If I can make it,
Tomorrow, I'll be five.

THE DYING GIRL

The dying girl
who lamented
the bite of people,
cherished
the politeness of vultures
who at least
wait their turn.

SYSTEMIC

Systemically Slaughtered

A pile of bodies charred and machine gunned
to gruesome mosaic.
Each piece of head bearing
silent hymns,
to deaf Heaven,
to blind God.

Systemically Hidden

Aggregate fresh denials.
Convenience sprouts the collective deceit,
birthing a half-truth in the mind
of harrowing events
made palatable
by the myth of progress.

Systemically Forgotten

Reinvent the murderer, to misguided neighbor,
without moral choice.
Relegate the victim
to faceless story.
Shade of an era,
from a long distance,
of minor years.

BLUE VALOR

A deformity of valor
before the Poe Poe drop the hammer,
pursuing the day's quota,
with a dance of fists
for questioning lips.

He's trying to resist!
preludes a song of bullets
sung, in the ongoing fable
of rights unread,
the blue in their head,
makes the whole ghetto red.

Explanations for the dead:
Resistance to authority,
A gathering crowd,
The deadliest minority.

White eyes in dark faces,
in spaces where "good folk"
should reign,
impoverished faces
unraveling white peace
with black pain.

A deformity of valor
before the Poe Poe drop the hammer,
chanting Blue Lives Matter!
in response to a war

the brutalized never asked for.
Grieving, widowed wives
for the love of Black lives.
Justice riots
when an innocent man dies.

PARABLE OF THE BLUE MAN

A Blue Man placed a pointed ear to one of the 41 holes he'd made in the skin of God's favorite black clothes.

"All I hear is havoc," he said, his voice unsteady.

"Listen deeper, past the rage."

"I hear his days, given little chance, but he's accountable for his behavior, he cannot claim happenstance." The Blue Man cursed, defiant.

God remained silent.

"I hear his tears born of his fears. But all men weep . . . What of my fears? These people aren't gentle sheep! He is the one who chose to live violently! God, why are you so silent?"

From within, God's voice rose, but it could've been conscience speaking, the Blue Man supposed.

"Is he the one to unmake you? Shatter you down to chains, scar the pride from your back, entomb you in lack? Did he fill your neighborhood with crack? Redline your hopes for a better dream? Enlist savagery as a theme for his image across your screen? Does he own the factories manufacturing the guns, killing his sons? Yet you fear him in monstrous ways. Shouldn't it be him who's terrified these days? Should he not refuse friendship every time you seek? Should he not doubt every word you speak?"

"Those are not my ways! I wasn't born in those days. Everyone struggles, we all face adversity! Some make it, and some fade away. You made this order. Isn't this your way?"

"Should the fading fade quietly? Or should they shout and roar? Shouldn't they take from your mouth and rage at your door?"

"Let them come! I'm ready! I put forty-one shots in this one already! Injustices happen! The past can't be changed, but I'll protect mines and what remains! The heritage of mines is not all spent, defined by the story your black clothes lent! There is love and glory and victories true, there is goodness in the story we've written in the name of you!"

"When much is taken, much is spent. The quality of the seed is the nature of the crop lent. Your ways are not my ways. Good does not wash away the bad. Gaze into the holes of your favors, see the future of your labors."

The Blue Man investigated one of the 41 holes he'd made, weary, knowing the truth is always scary. He saw visions of an empire's fading glory on a foundation of red. Its legacy was unsteady in the storms of time. Cain and Abel replayed with both brothers slain. Blood on each other's hands. "Am I my brother's keeper?" Replayed again and again on the lips of unaccountable men. Sins dealt for sins wagered. Injustice accepted in the name of dominant skin.

Every shade of God's clothes was full of holes, leaking a rainbow of tragic colors.

The Blue Man convulsed in revulsion. His eyes were wet with history's tears. Looking up higher than his justifications had ever allowed, he searched for God's true face behind the mask he'd sculpted to suit his own reflection. And then, for the first time in his life, he asked her sincerely,

"Lord, how do I fix this?"

And things began to change.

HARMLESS

The Harmless Man creates a clever myth
to shame the will to fight,
slandering virtue
with downcast eyes,
shoulders dominated by gravity,
placid smile,
performative morality.

This species of the harmless,
a race of self-traitors
who caged the inner beast,
accepting the slap,
turning the other cheek.
Submitting,
whichever way the pain-wind blows,
cupping their noses
to mitigate the stench
of unused souls.

Endless compromise, rationalized.
Pretending to be meek.
In the face of injustice, unable to speak.
Fearing to die, unable to live.
Fearing to love, unable to give.
Without the will to kill,
to stand as a man,
none can inspire evil,
as the Harmless Man can.

DON'T YOU SEE?

23

Without meaning, his life
minor glories,
laborious nothings,
sand in open fingers.

Death reversed his fortunes.
Come closer,
peer into eyes
made dry
where little flies dance.

See?

Maggots
taste the taster.
The whole mouth
a bloated stage.

Internal performers,
Broadway within the meat
we hide beneath the dirt.

How beautiful his stillness,
the utter disregard of want.
Finally, greed-less,
he gives selflessly to lesser things.

Serene in the dreaming
of longest night,
I witness
the nobility in his rot.
Inhale, the putrid evaporation
of his inequities . . .

Look . . .

Don't you see?

There are no meaningless deaths.

IS THIS DEATH?

"Is this death?"

Entangled trumpets usher
a hideous heat,
echoing,
as if from the throat
of shrieking crones.

The baleful judgement,
scorching,
from vistas unseen,
laments the guiding error,
my bloodless regret.

I stand skinless
in daunting feebleness,
eyeless witness
to the decrepit value
of a wasted human soul.

"Is this death?"

Manic, my plea,
a pebble in the shadow
of galaxies,
graveyard and cradle
to a petty God.

Mewling infant,
this limbless I Am,
infantile in its smallness.
Confronted by the wasteful,
utterly wasteful, idea of Me.

"Is this death?"

His voice,
source of ceaseless
trumpeting heat,
transverses black eternities to smother
the meager embers of dreams:

"Salvation."

THE SILENCE OF GOD

Words.
The original dream.
Upon his tongue,
. . . *Tasted* . . .
Unseen.

Wet words.
Forced through
Bacteria-caked spaces.
. . . *Behold* . . .
His bloody teeth.

Aged words.
Death, his lips.
Pass,
Kissed,
. . . *Drifting* . . .
Unseen.

Lost words.
Without from within.
Not his children,
Nor his kin.
Are we
. . . *the answer* . . .
. . . *or the scream* . . .
The tears
in God's

      dream?

HOW DEVOLUTION STARTS

The worst *Me* found the best *You.*
This is how devolution starts:
An immovable object
meeting an unstoppable force
and having sex with it.

The first decides to woefully inch forward,
the second decides to stop, in a comfortable dream of routine.
Logic implodes, reason unravels to nonsensical justifications
within a personal dystopia of *Us.*

The love of my worst and your best makes the whole world flat,
an asymmetrical dark forest of wounds, salted by, *"Let me
explain."*

Your worn body vacates our burning galaxy of wrong,
leaving behind the remnants of another broken heart,
orbiting the black hole of my soul.

MEDICINE

I just
want you to know,
as I lie in the company of pus,
dying in a most unpleasant way, without
the cheap vanity of friends, that I will get better,
simply to outlive you.

Yes, life is not a race, but death is a game of chase, of hide
and seek, as it both hides and seeks. I must live long enough, to
point, until you're found.

O, to see Death pop out your favorite cake, to see your tongue
hang gray,
the whites of your eyes farming maggots.

To slander your memory, with the secrets confided in me,
creating
splendid doubt in those who loved you, laughing hysterically,
at your final moments of need.

Suffer as I've suffered, knowing the same air allows you
to breathe. Perish on the hill of loathsome burdens,
Moon-howling eccentric agonies . . .

O, Creator! O, Maker! For this, splendid this,
I will take my
medicine.

PINK BANANA

Observing similarities
in the phallus
and her favorite fruit,
she gripped the root.

With the fruit knife,
peeled skin
to hanging flaps,
at the side
of bloody pink.

Screams, ceaseless.
But for her, a smile.

This would be unlike
any smoothie
she'd blended before.

GORGON FRUIT

Solemn
feast of petrification,
reaching shadows, numb
antiquated forms angled
to tragic light,
in sight
of setting sun.

Voiceless,
their moaning,
in Masonic gray.
Dreadful moss on sunken pool,
in empty paths
of day.

Heaving,
the still breathing
in stone,
pigments morphed
rustic white,
all life, akin to bone.

Haughtily,
the haunted hunger,
glory, to blossomed doom,
stillness
of deepest time,
in roots
of shadowed moon.

Echoes,
noosed on loathsome branches,
strange fruit, centered,

with lidless eye,
demanding the gorging
of graying meat,
from those who fear to die.

A FRUIT CALLED WRATH

Bellona pretended not to see
    the one who waited.
    Her second shadow,
    rising to rightful stature,
Whenever her husband's fists rattled the bones of her face.

She wobbled on her legs now, by the familiar tree,
unsure what parts of the wetness were blood or tears.
Those useless tears, which changed nothing.
    The shadow at the corner of her vision
    beckoned in night whispers.

    "Consider the children."
Bellona's heart throbbed painfully,
wicked hopes of a miracle
burned to spiritual ash, ungraspable.
    "Consider the children."

She remembered his strong hands,
squeezing the juice from her neck,
drop by drop, into a bucket of strained pleas.
"Not in front of the girls!" she had begged.
"Please . . . don't let them see . . . "

In the delirium of the moment,
the frenzied flailing of hands and feet,
her daughters screaming,
the oldest, just seven, Camilla,
ran over and bit her father's thigh as hard as she could.

He kicked the little girl in turn,
sending her rolling in a small ball of limbs,
across the living room floor.

And the monster, still thinking himself a man,
let Bellona drop in a heap.

He stared at the grief of his daughters,
one sobbing against a wall,
the other hidden beneath the kitchen table.
"You see what you make me do!" he roared,
vomit-breath smelling of liquor.

"Sorry," he uttered, then he remembered himself.
"Camilla! Do that again, and I'll straighten you out like your
mother. Little bitch!"
He lumbered off, as if proud,
into the night of the woods.
Not gone. Never gone.

   "Consider the children.
   "What will they become?
   "What will they allow?"
Bellona looked to the darkness.
"Who are you?"

   "Daughter, don't you recognize your own rage?"
"What is your name?"
   "All names feminine. All faces fair.
   "Bearer of the world.
   "Caretaker of thy wrath."

Bellona felt a primordial hunger
pouring from the shadow woman into herself.
Fury ushered her fully into the shadows,
where what was blurred came into focus.
She saw the shadow woman wore her face.

   "What becomes of a man's violations upon a woman's
    flesh?
   "Don't we bear them in the womb of our pain?
   "Don't we give until we're empty, our dreams sacrificed
    for their children's joy?
   "We bear the burden of life, and still they bring us death.

"Daughter, tell me: Where do the sins of men dwell
when the world forgets them?"

"They gather in the soil of a garden empty of mothers.
"Where they coalesce into a seed watered by our sisters' tears.
"They grow a tree of obsidian bark and honey-gold leaves.
"The tree harvests the pain of the greater half of the world . . .
and bears a fruit called Wrath."
"I am the fruit of that tree. You and me."

She knew where to go
to gather the pitchfork from the garden,
divining its many uses.
She put the kids to bed
promising a new morning.

Only Camilla suspected,
a gleam in her eye,
of Valkyrie's hue,
approving of what mother
had to do.

The monster returned
and called her to his bed.
Bellona went,
placing the pitchfork
where he could not see.

It was her fault,
he said as fact,
while indulging in gentle touch.
Oh, how he loved her,
but her mouth was too much.

Bellona kissed her husband
to settle him to rest.
She did her best to temper
the shadow in her chest,
a kraken of rage, begging for blood and flesh.

Shadow hands
helped guide the pitchfork
to its proper place,
into his eyes, his groin,
and his face.

The litany of screams
as if from her wildest dreams,
wonderfully burdened,
with magnificent pleas.
        "Think of the children."

Bellona also thought of herself,
and her own avengement.
Poking the monster again and again,
till her passions scattered chunks of his head,
in mangled pieces, upon the bed.

        "Be free, daughter. You and me."
Sitting upon the gore, red-stained in peace,
Bellona released all thoughts of the slaughtered,
resting serenely within the hope of a family,
unburdened by the wants of men.

        "Be free."

All evil was born,
in innocence,
and chose.

A BLACK SCREAM IN THE TWILIGHT

Much can be said on the in-between places where thought and feeling converge to try and make sense of the totality of the self. The good, the bad, the ugly, and the sad. They coalesce at the border of contradiction, reflecting our humanity.

The works in this section are confessions of vulnerability. They explore the grim beauty inherent in the touch of light and shadows.

TWILIGHT SONATA

What darkness wounds, light heals.
What light heals, twilight steals.

The last sunbeams,
in-between the swaying dreams of leaves,
sing a golden lullaby to grass,
as shadows
watch the warmth pass.

Purple, orange, pink-traced gold,
a sky of flowers,
dark blue, bold.

Before the sun gives a final kiss
to the horizon's lips,
in-between somehow and now,

The conquering stars look down,
and know us.

EARLY LIES

Ask me anything,
but spare me
everything
you mean to say.
"How are you doing?"
First lie of the day.

SONGS OF YOUTH

We
cannot
sing the songs
we sung
when we were young.

Gone, the selfsame delight
of the unweighted heart,

with the spark of fresh soul,
awash in the soil
of promised flowers,

bright-eyed wonders,
pondering
the playful science
of what we will be,

until decades
of failings
make us
see.

WE CHANGE

44

Sometimes it's I love you.
We change.

Sometimes its I hate you.
We change.

Always it's I need, I want, I deserve.
Always it's me, sometimes you.

We hope to change
what has never changed.
The long delay, pretending day
will not bring night.

We change the name
but not the fight.

We change the hope
but not the behavior.

The allegory of the cave
in darkness, reorganizing the
same tools, painting over
the same wall.

Changing nothing
but the colors
we pretend to see.

I'M SORRY

I know nothing more wicked
than the heart of the animal,
fortified inside
the unrepentant self.

In baleful conceit it gnaws,
a soliloquy in whispered ear,
creating fine excuses
for every terror
I condemned another to wear.

Why must we despise those who try to love us?

As you prayed for my misery,
So, did I pray.

As you scuttled from my mercies,
So, did I scuttle.

As you betrayed,
So, did I betray.

The hiding can be done in bluster and pomp,
tears can be found in a coward's convictions,
strength is cruelty in a fool.

See now, the mirror of me,
underneath the fluff,
the pus smells of nectar.

We were young, so it's sung,
Oh, the generous lies we tell,
to appease the Hells I crafted

for the innocent.

Solemn are the choices,
my lips refuse to tell.

I stand as you stood,
divorced of forgiveness.

I yearn as you've yearned,
without the courage to return.

I lament as you've lamented,
fearing the chance to say,

"I'm sorry."

ALONE

Everyone I love leaves.
I cannot trust the promises of
lovers or brothers,
sisters or friends.
Unreasonable, my ends,
stubborn in my mistrust.
Why am I never good enough?
At least in death the promise remains true,
even I
can abandon me, too.

HELP ME

Help me hate you.
Say the things unsaid,
slaughter love's delusion
to coffins, dead.

Torment me to freedom.
Baptisms in shame.
Tell me your whats
without your whys,
half-truths in self-righteous lies.

Absolve me of self-respect,
don't leave anything precious
left to protect.
Show me an end,
where I can't pretend.

Crucified in a ditch,
beneath the soil
of a 'better' you,
convince yourself
it's true,
that I never
loved you, too.

GOODBYE

The
gavel
came down.
Grown-up voices
speak hopeless words,
condemning the heart of I,
the child, crying.

They would not let me go to mommy,
so, I reached with eight-year-old hands,
willing to separate my shoulder from every
tendon, to join the tips of our tears.

I, reaching; she, saying, *"It's going to be okay."*

A child can grieve the entire world in a second,
and keeps grieving, long after every cell is new.

I, reaching; she, smiling; Mommy's face the first sunrise,
eyes dripping waterfalls; her voice, my first melody.

Promising we can return to playgrounds, where, as Icarus, I rode
the clouds with wings, the rusty creaking of the swings mingling
with my giggling, the kissing wind making poverty disappear.

I, reaching, till our fingertips almost touch, my
eight-year-old arms not strong enough.

She, drifting away: *"It's going to be okay."*

Never, not ever, or again,
will I allow . . .
weakness.

FOSTER CARE

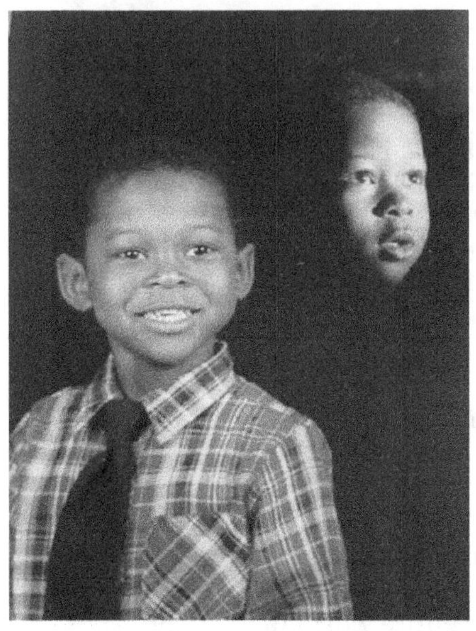

My first meditation took place in a corner,
when I was seven years old,
on a stranger's floor.
I would not call her mother,
that's what they killed me for.

The innocent me, who loved gummy bears,
and Sunday morning cartoons,
who read his bible,
who thought he could breakdance on the moon.

At least it's not my little brother.
I can endure,
enough for both of us,
endure, endure . . .

Electric wire can cut skin better than a knife,
each lash,
each cry of shame,
telling me boys don't cry,
stripping me of my name.

Becoming pain,
no longer innocent of hate,
it's too late, God, it's too late,
to be good.

Endure, endure.
This will be my life.
Unloved in fright,
a little black thing undeserving.
This will be my life.

Lashes with blame,
hatred.
Terrible hatred.
And unanswered prayers.

I discover my pride,
if my blood can't hide,
so, my defiance must be seen.

"Stupid little nigger!"

Blood on a stranger's floor.
I endure.
In a corner, dreaming of mother.

WHO YOU BECAME

It can't happen to me,
Becomes, why did it happen to me?
Becomes, it shouldn't have happened to me.
Becomes, why didn't it happen to you?
Becomes, it should have happened to you.
Becomes, I'm going to do it to you!
Becomes, you deserve it . . .
Becomes,
who
     you
          became.

INTENTIONS

I see my intentions,
I see your actions,
I judge
You.
I condemn
You.
I forgive
Me.

Attracting
The heartbeat
Of life's
Disappointments.
My life
Is wife
To mayhem.

I fear,
I banish,
I blame.
Shame does not
Touch my pride.
Eyes wide,
Seeing everything
But mercy.

I hide
Inside
Behind
Moral disdain.

Hating
Nameless faces
Conceptualized
In blame.

This shame,
O, this shame,
If they could
Only see
My
Intentions!

Forgive!
Judge me not,
As I
Have judged
You.

*I must see beyond my own knowledge
to the unknowable truth
on the far side of unlearning.
Knowing nothing,
I am free.*

A SONG OF DAWN

The light is Life. Direct it through the prism of love, and see it divide into the colors of Truth, Hope, and Harmony. Illumination of the heart and the head, transforming pain into beauty.

The pieces in this section are about honesty. What makes us all human from a perspective of joy, not cynicism. It asks questions, explores feelings, and justifies dreams.

OR PERHAPS . . .

Perhaps, Love is the motive,
Perhaps, Hope creates Fate,
Perhaps, your faith is Prosperity's gate.

Perhaps, every day we get to choose Heaven,
Perhaps, the church invented Hell,
Perhaps, Death is nothing but a revelation too sweet to tell.

Perhaps, everything you love is more real than how you feel.
Perhaps, at the end of the day, fear is not such a big deal.

Perhaps, pain is the mother of beauty,
Perhaps, what hurts connects you to all souls.
Perhaps, you get to choose what makes you whole.

Perhaps, we are the midwives of higher intelligences to come,
Perhaps, givers are having the most fun.

Perhaps, the haters are right!
Perhaps, you pray for them before you sleep at night.
Perhaps, I inspired you, got around your despair,
Perhaps, God's love is greater than your fear.

Perhaps this and perhaps that,
Perhaps,
Life is the only true fact.

Or perhaps . . .

MERCY IS HOPE AND HEALING

No one will ever know the violence it took
to become this gentle.

The cruelty it took to become this kind.

Letting go did not remove the knife . . .

The slow pull, the screaming
and gnashing of teeth,
blood given for blood spilt.

To pick at the self, one bite at a time,

My wrongs embedded
deep as marrow, sins deep as blood,
circulate in shriveled spirit,
deprived of love.

From a corpse, this man flowered
from a broken, willful husk.

Living to suffer,
I had to die to live.

Forgive if not forgiven.
This new living,
mercy is hope and healing.

STAY. LIVE.

When you can't die,
but you don't have the courage
to live.
When breathing pains
the soul,
and healing opens wounds.

Do not obey
the call to relief,
the grieving escape,
plummeting to concrete.

Stay.
It is a blender, not an abyss.
On and off again,
grinding us all to
compassion's paste.
All our tears bear the same
salty taste.

Stay.
What you feel is real.
You are the feeler,
behind the feeling,
the believer behind the dream,
the unseen chooser, choosing the seen.

Stay.
Find yourself a better story
behind the face of another,
invest your smiles
in the relief of a stranger.

Stay.
The agony inside you,
reverberates
in the shared quilt
of the human experience,
billions strong,
with billions yet to be born.

Live.
You'll find we're more the same,
in the endless tides of uncertainty,
drifting together, never quite apart.
It has been this way since the start,
before our time,
the distance between hearts,
bridged by pain,
redeemed through love,
cleaning our guilt and our shame.

Live.
We can heal generations,
if we have the courage to endure
a little more,
beyond an ending we can't see.
If we find the will to be,
simply be,
the You within Me.

A GIFT OF ILLNESS

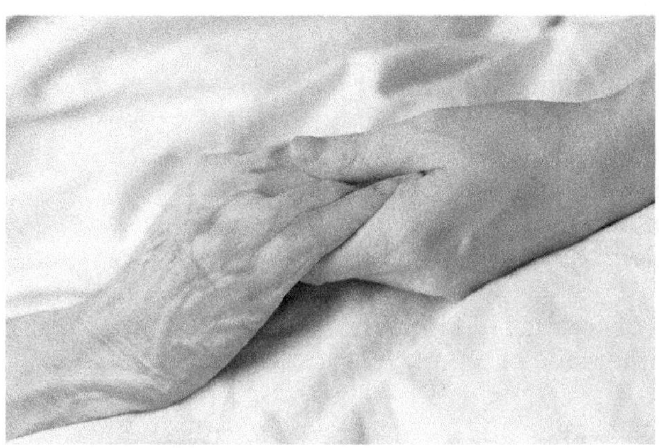

—The rustle of a sheet. The nurse smiles down at me—

I've been put on notice.
There is no forever in this form.
Skin never deserved my worship,
sickness has made that plain.
We become rational in the slow dying,
it's in the living when we are less than sane.

—The steady beeping of machines. The I.V. in my skin—

I will not fade peacefully,
unknowing and sudden.
I must linger now, take my bow.
Disheveled, deformed,
but not undone.

—Deep breaths of the ventilator—

Pain loosens lips,
grief opens ears,
our reasons made plain.
Love suddenly seen

by the blindest of the stubborn.
What cost, my malice?
How wasteful, utterly wasteful,
the time apart.

—The creak of an opening door. Eager footsteps—

Beautifully, they gather,
faces brightened by the memory of my life,
shedding tears in honor
of the road traveled, the contribution shared.
All the vile fears
are precious acts of courage left unmet,
a dream on the other side of regret.
These last days,
in a spiritually dead age,
are the final religion.

*—Hands intertwine, while the little hand of a child gently
caresses an ear—*

Thank the growths.
Thank the cough.
Thank the shortness of breath.
Thank the fading light.
Me, the blessed sufferer,
of failing flesh,
caressed to gladness by Death's own hand,
to live a lifetime, in the length of a breath . . .

EVERYBODY DIES

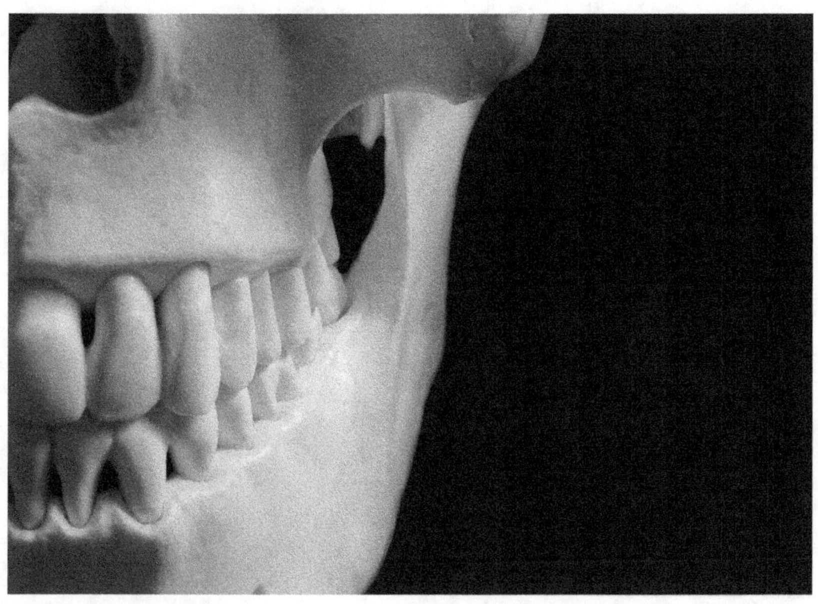

In the end, everybody dies.
Sorry to spoil the ending,
To ruin the surprise.

The good, the bad,
The certain, the sad,
The vegan whose eaten an egg or two,
The gluten free (*is that you?*)

The Atkins diet, discreet,
Eating the testis, the marrow, and the meat.
All their skeletons look the same,
Bleach white, once death came.

In the end, everybody dies.
Sorry to spoil the ending,
To ruin the surprise.

As rich as you were
As proud as you were,
All the countries you've seen,
Whether or not you achieved your dream.

In faith or in fiction,
On a toilet or a bed,
Death comes a-knocking
        With its own plans instead.

No need to cry that life ain't fair.
Death is fair, to the point of fear,
So beware,
        or not.
It'll find you all the same,
        in sleet or sheet, in comfort or pain.

Everybody dies.
In the end, we're all the same.
Our choices matter
        in the same way they do not.
This is our moment
To breathe, to love,
To narrate the plot.

It's the true, true.
One day, we'll all be dead,
        but for now,
Embrace this thing called living,
You're breathing instead!

YOUR LIFE

There will be faces, many faces with mouths, and the mouths will have words, and the words will have opinions, about your opinions, about your actions, about your non-actions, and all the things you should've been.

A dark forest of mouths attached to faces you once enjoyed.

The belligerent noise of their panic will strike a mace against your cranium, race a fiery chariot across your brain, sowing seeds of a barbed texture,
growing as you do, till out, out, out, blossom the slimy roots of doubt.

Don't contort your spirit in painful configuration, no capitulation! Hold the line, it's only for a lifetime, one brief life. *Your* life,

That's the important thing.

HER, SELF

At the crux of the self,
she stepped over her old life,
for it was a rotting thing,
owned by memory.

Pride rose from its cobweb veins,
vanity rooted to its pain,
all the justifications, dead.

As Athena,
birthing herself,
as *Isis*,
knowing herself,
regrowing
from her head.

Only the scars she kept,
and the dreams, somehow new,
into the distant place forward . . .
that only phoenixes knew.

HER NAME

She is bioluminescent
with the gifts of morning,
transforming
her rainbow mien
to nourishing life.
She says it tastes like sunlight,
it feels of moon,
She says, soon,
we can be Earth's treasure.

I place her symbols of rose and jasmine,
of lotus, with male seed,
on fertility's alter.
She bleeds,
with the promise to give,
guarding the gate
where futures live.

Sometimes, I despise her
to hide the suffering of my pride.
I have nothing to provide
that she needs.
Though I build and build,
she builds the builders,

though I fight and war,
she restores.

The sublime moment of my undoing
is in her choosing.
In her arms, I am tasted,
weighed and measured,
desired and pleasured.
A new world,
soul-deep inside,
liberated from the graveyard
of my boyish pride.

She doesn't need to kill,
but does so,
in her own way.
Turning a house into a home,
potential into a meal,
power into strength,
a *hope* . . . into something real.

I sing the songs!
I am the warmth beside her.
I'll be her protector and provider.
Heaven knows,
Eden will never be the same,

Woman is her name.

KYEISHA & NICK

Tender are the feet of love,
on the long coals of fire,
each step a revelation towards
a paradox
of two hearts,
two lives,
two choices,
becoming one fact.

We search the world for ourselves,
already ourselves,

we search the world for love,
already loved.

Here we find wholeness.
Two souls,
complete in their singular fullness,
orbiting each other like binary stars
to illuminate a galaxy manifested
by choice.

In their choosing,
they have combined their light:
brilliant, beautiful, and warm.

In their choosing,
they have given us delights to taste,
hopes to hear, and a lifelong dream to watch,
reinforcing the purpose of love
in the commitment of their smiles.

Tiny constellations have appeared.
Sublime Kayiah and passionate Nathan.
The embodiment of a magic,
scientifically defined but impossible to explain.

Tender are the feet of love
on the long coals of fire,
and tender may they remain
whether walking on glass,
in fear or in pain,
tender may your love remain,
warm before all ice,
growing deeper, while remaining firm.

Help us all to learn as you learn,
to eternally be, the beauty that we see,
in this moment of two YOUs
as one WE.

SANCTIONED

Sanction
means to allow
and not to allow.

The moments sanctioned,
happened.

The moments sanctioned,
you chose.

Living a resumé of life
sanctioned by choice.

By love,

By hope,

By experiences of change,
remains
the sanctioned road
to peace.

THE BRIDGE ABOVE THEIR WALLS

What was done, I did not become . . .

By Heaven's Grace,
I walked the road of broken glass,
leaving crimson trails
on forgiveness' path.

My wrath surrendered,
I deny resentment of my soul,
my labors, my goals!
To declare above their walls:

What was done, I did not become . . .

The unfairness suffered,
though the heart grieves,
it bleeds a testament,
redeemed by my crucible,
leaving no further offerings
to their cycles of hate.

What was done, I did not become . . .

In beauty's joyous ache,
what becomes,
my attention creates.

BUTTERFLY WINGS

Butterflies
cannot see
their own wings,

Beauty often hides
from its bearer's eyes,

Radiant as the soul sings,
Soft, as butterfly wings,

As watchers' hearts flutter
to life's gift, chastening time.

If even one is divine, all are saved.
If beauty is courageous, all love is brave.

Beauty, the road where redemptions
are paved.

All this, a secret, for you
and for me,

The butterfly floats,
unable
to see . . .

WAVES

Soul sings the ocean river,
poised waves
      sparkle,
         shimmer.

Precious cycle,
rhythmic,
        mirror.

Live,
    give,
      take.

Salt taste,
scent of rain,
    mystery's depth,
      history of breath.

    All that changes,
      must change,
In you,
I am Earth-blood,
    one droplet
       of
endless
    spring.

IN THE RIGHT

I would rather be right
than do the right thing.

That's the beginning
of our tears.

The sorrow in your eyes
is my only prize,
when the dust settles.

Inebriated on this battle-
wrecked right,
uplifting a fragmented
theory,

I need you to accept,
to make me real.

Oh God,
I could love you,
if only I was wrong.

THE FOOL'S SLUMBER

Engulfed in knowing's fire,
Point the barrel of reason,
Pull hard the desperate trigger,
Your shooting logic
Strikes the fool in the head,
Missing the entire brain,
Where the fool remains,
Astride soft pillows,
In peaceful reign
Over happy lands
Wisdom will never touch.

MOMMY MAGIC

I can ride the back of Pegasus,
trotting hoofprints
on a cloud,
melt Smaug's treasure
into a golden trapeze,
for a silver clown, dancing around
with his bronze flute,
jollying a tune,
climbing Jack's beanstalk
to Seuss' green moon.
I can use all three wishes,
before you make me do the dishes,
dodge Martian lasers quicker
than an off-to-school kiss,
but the spell I can't resist
is the magic
of your smile.

I love you, Mommy.

SIBLINGS

We must admit the gift of siblings
is sweeter when it goes away,
teaching us to appreciate distance,
and the humble joys each day.

You love 'em because Momma told you to.
You commit to liking them,
but that's even harder than liking *you*.

Yet, here we go again,
on holidays or random invasions *(visits)*,
reverting to behaviors you thought you outgrew,
setting traps to let everyone know
they're not impressed by you.

That they'll refuse to listen,
or let you get your way,
'cause you are THEIRS,
in the possessive,
and you must NEVER win the day.

Condemned to a silent competition,
with self-esteem keeping score,
What's it all for?
What's it all for!

This relationship, longest in a life,
perpetual strife,
cold wars behind awkward smiles . . .
Nitpicking every flaw,
with each transformation
at the front door.

But a witness to this life,
obligated to grieve.
To love, to need.
To open their door when the world is burning.
To call each screw-up an act of learning.

To give context to the pain when it's all gone insane,
holding our wrinkled hand at the end,
my sibling, my enemy, my friend.

HAPPY BIRTHDAY

Another cycle in the spiral
of love's destined day.
Manifested by the unbroken chain
of generations, who found a way.

Another cycle within the miracle
of breathing.
Believing in the gift of life,
beyond the limits
of imperfect sight.

Embracing this brief node
of mine
in the chain of time.
Seeking the part of you
awakened in the divine.

Nothing but gratitude on this day,
sculpted by faith's own hand.
Happy Birthday! Happy Birthday!!

Here I stand.

RESTORATION

By Jamal Hodge & Kyeisha Hodge

The haunting child
reaches
for the face of the adult,
reaching
for the meaning
carved into darkness.

Ravaged pieces of light
leave life an unchanged despair.
I can no longer hear

When the Cherubim sings.
My stride resides in darkness,
where all angels lose their wings.

Where is the kingdom of the righteous?
Who celebrates the meek?
Our past dooming our future ways,
how long can the spirit endure evil days?

The haunting child
reaches,
untouched by time,
speaking divine comedy,
within this lost face of mine.

Into me I see,
an unbroken chain
of a thousand lifetimes,
leading to my name,

—Despite—
The fear.

—Despite—
The blood paid.

—Despite—
This mundane charade.

Providing the greatest luxury,
a LIFE, beyond circumstance,
my life,
in wisdom's light,

I reach
with the child, reaching,
seeking,

Restored.

*What am I that dreams,
this dreaming
of me?*

I am only what I am.

THE END?

Not if you want to dive into more of Crystal Lake Publishing's Tales from the Darkest Depths!

Check out our amazing website and online store
or download our latest catalog here.
https://geni.us/CLPCatalog

We always have great new projects and content on the website to dive into, as well as a newsletter, behind the scenes options, social media platforms, our own dark fiction shared-world series and our very own webstore. Our webstore even has categories specifically for KU books, non-fiction, anthologies, and of course more novels and novellas.

ABOUT THE AUTHOR

Jamal Hodge is a native New Yorker who grew up surrounded by the perils of poverty, the diversity of convergent cultures, and the harmonious circus of six siblings. He is a multi-award-winning film director, a two-time Rhysling Award nominee, and a 2nd place Dwarf Stars award-winning poet, whose one obsession is exploring the great "Why?" inside each of us.

Jamal loves the broken things that want to be understood and the secret things that never bothered to hide. With his writing, he hopes to uncover the paradox between suffering and meaning, to use darkness to show light.

When he's not writing or filming, Jamal is traveling to odd locales, volunteering at some community organization, or in the gym working out to a near death experience.

He fancies himself a pretty cool guy.

COPYRIGHT ACKNOWLEDGEMENTS

The Great Blue Stomach That Circles The Sun (Published in *Space & Time Magazine*, Issue 134, 2019)

Tomorrow I'll Be Five (Published in *Whispers From Beyond*, Crystal Lake Publishing 2024)

Parable Of The Blue Man (Published in *Chiral Mad Anthology V5*, Written Backwards 2022)

The Silence of God (*HWA Poetry Showcase Volume 8*, 2021)

Pink Banana (*The Siren's Call Issue 58*, Summer 2022)

GorgonFruit (*Penumbric* issue, December 2023)

Readers . . .

Thank you for reading *The Dark Between the Twilight*. We hope you enjoyed this poetry collection.

If you have a moment, please review *The Dark Between the Twilight* at the store where you bought it.

Help other readers by telling them why you enjoyed this book. No need to write an in-depth discussion. Even a single sentence will be greatly appreciated. Reviews go a long way to helping a book sell, and is great for an author's career. It'll also help us to continue publishing quality books.

Thank you again for taking the time to journey with Crystal Lake Publishing.

Visit our Linktree page for a list of our social media platforms.
https://linktr.ee/CrystalLakePublishing

Follow us on Amazon:

Our Mission Statement:

Since its founding in August 2012, Crystal Lake Publishing has quickly become one of the world's leading publishers of Dark Fiction and Horror books. In 2023, Crystal Lake Publishing formed a part of Crystal Lake Entertainment, joining several other divisions, including Torrid Waters, Crystal Lake Comics, Crystal Lake Kids, and many more.

While we strive to present only the highest quality fiction and entertainment, we also endeavour to support authors along their writing journey. We offer our time and experience in non-fiction projects, as well as author mentoring and services, at competitive prices.

With several Bram Stoker Award wins and many other wins and nominations (including the HWA's Specialty Press Award), Crystal Lake Publishing puts integrity, honor, and respect at the forefront of our publishing operations.

We strive for each book and outreach program we spearhead to not only entertain and touch or comment on issues that affect our readers, but also to strengthen and support the Dark Fiction field and its authors.

Not only do we find and publish authors we believe are destined for greatness, but we strive to work with men and women who endeavour to be decent human beings who care more for others than themselves, while still being hard working, driven, and passionate artists and storytellers.

Crystal Lake Publishing is and will always be a beacon of what passion and dedication, combined with overwhelming teamwork and respect, can accomplish. We endeavour to know each and every one of our readers, while building personal relationships with our authors, reviewers, bloggers, podcasters, bookstores, and libraries.

We will be as trustworthy, forthright, and transparent as any business can be, while also keeping most of the headaches away from our authors, since it's our job to solve the problems so they can stay in a creative mind. Which of course also means paying our authors.

We do not just publish books, we present to you worlds within your world, doors within your mind, from talented authors who sacrifice so much for a moment of your time.

There are some amazing small presses out there, and through collaboration and open forums we will continue to support other presses in the goal of helping authors and showing the world what quality small presses are capable of accomplishing. No one wins when a small press goes down, so we will always be there to support hardworking, legitimate presses and their authors. We don't see Crystal Lake as the best press out there, but we will always strive to be the best, strive to be the most interactive and grateful, and even blessed press around. No matter what happens over time, we will also take our mission very seriously while appreciating where we are and enjoying the journey.

What do we offer our authors that they can't do for themselves through self-publishing?

We are big supporters of self-publishing (especially hybrid publishing), if done with care, patience, and planning. However, not every author has the time or inclination to do market research, advertise, and set up book launch strategies. Although a lot of authors are successful in doing it all, strong small presses will always be there for the authors who just want to do what they do best: write.

What we offer is experience, industry knowledge, contacts and trust built up over years. And due to our strong brand and trusting fanbase, every Crystal Lake Publishing book comes with weight of respect. In time our fans begin to trust our judgment and will try a new author purely based on our support of said author.

With each launch we strive to fine-tune our approach, learn from our mistakes, and increase our reach. We continue to assure our authors that we're here for them and that we'll carry the weight of the launch and dealing with third parties while they focus on their strengths—be it writing, interviews, blogs, signings, etc.

We also offer several mentoring packages to authors that include knowledge and skills they can use in both traditional and self-publishing endeavours.

We look forward to launching many new careers.

This is what we believe in. What we stand for. This will be our legacy.

Welcome to Crystal Lake Publishing— Tales from the Darkest Depths.

www.ingramcontent.com/pod-product-compliance
Lightning Source LLC
Chambersburg PA
CBHW050955050726
47592CB00007B/2576